CW00429931

AT LEAST ONE GOAL!

THE WINNING STRATEGY ON OVER 0.5

Pavel Nowak

WARNING

Warning: The unauthorized reproduction or distribution of this copyrighted work is illegal. No part of this book may be scanned, uploaded, or distributed via the internet or other means, electronic or print without the author's permission. Criminal copyright infringement without monetary gain is investigated by the FBI and is punishable by up to 5 years in federal prison. Please purchase only authorized electronic or print editions and do not participate in or encourage the electronic piracy of this copyrighted material.

LEGAL & DISCLAIMER

Continuing with this reading, the user is aware of and agrees that: The Author of this Book does not intend to provide any financial advice or encourage gambling, nor does he consider himself responsible in any way for the consequences and choices of anyone who reads his books.

Any information contained in the following Book is for educational and instructional purposes only.

There is no direct or indirect advertising of Gambling in any way.

TABLE OF CONTENTS

INTRODUCTION

Here we are, welcome back! Are you ready to study my top strategy on Over 0.5?

In this book, we won't just talk about predictions and theory. Instead, we'll provide numerous practical examples and include several images for reference. So, don't worry, this won't be one of those typical betting scam manuals you come across. Here, we delve into the specifics of professional betting on Over 0.5, covering everything from A to Z.

But before we begin, have you read my book "The Perfect Prediction"? You can find it on Amazon. In that book, you'll find a quick and comprehensive explanation of how to make accurate and effective predictions for football matches, including markets such as Over 0.5, Over 1.5, Both Teams to Score, Under 2.5, and Home Team Win. Since I plan to write dedicated books for each of these five markets, if you're reading this book without having read the introductory one, "The Perfect Prediction," I strongly recommend doing so to prepare yourself for reading this and all the other dedicated manuals.

As for me, if you don't know who I am, all you need to know for now is that I've been earning a living from betting for many years, consistently generating thousands of pounds each month...

I mention this to reassure you that it is absolutely true that you can make a living from betting, and I know this for certain because both myself and several of my colleagues have been doing so without too many difficulties.

In short, making money through betting is possible!

And you are here to make money, right?

So, focus on making money and learning to bet. That's it. To accelerate your learning process, it may be helpful to think about what you want to achieve with the money you will win through betting. (It's better to know this from the start so that you have a clear direction and objective in mind!).

I'm not ashamed to tell you that initially, my strong desire that drove me to become extremely skilled in betting was the ability to afford spending time with models (even in a paid manner). In practice, the driving force that brought me here was the desire to have a great time with beautiful Eastern European women in an elegant hotel downtown.

Then, once I achieved my dreams of being with the women I desired, fortunately, I realized that there was more to do with the money I earned, so I started making investments (now I have even more money to spend on Russian escorts).

What I want to tell you is that you need to focus on what you want to achieve even before starting to study and bet...

When it comes to betting, it's much better to be simple, direct, and clear with yourself (especially during the learning phase).

So, if you're reading this book, it's because you still haven't been able to achieve what you want through betting money. Or perhaps you're still in the phase where you're losing money... Probably, the reason for all this is that you haven't fully focused on your purpose.

Well, focus on your goals and keep your dream in mind. It will help you overcome difficult times. Above all, it will help you blindly follow your plan, your new strategy on Over 0.5, which I will teach you in detail and will prevent you from veering off course (which is the real problem for losing bettors).

You need maximum concentration to move on to the next chapter and discover the secrets of Over 0.5. Are you ready?

CONSIDERATIONS ON OVER

I have already touched upon the topic of "predictions" and how to predict various Over markets in my previous book, "The Perfect Prediction," so I won't dwell too much on the basics. However, I do want to provide you with a brief summary on the subject...

So, when studying a match with the aim of predicting the most probable market, there are two rules to always keep in mind:

1 Not all matches can be predicted, only a few, very few, after thorough analysis.

2 It should be the numbers and statistical probabilities that tell us which prediction to choose, not the other way around! (In other words, it's not us deciding which prediction is the most likely, but the statistics telling us.)

Therefore, when approaching an analysis of a match, a game that will be played in the coming days, the first thing to verify is whether it is a PREDICTABLE match. In other words, it should be an OBVIOUS match that doesn't involve too many surprises once it starts, and above all, a match that expresses a clear and evident direction through statistical numbers, indicating how it will most likely end.

The only way to analyze a match professionally, in order to come up with the best possible prediction, is to analyze it for what it is:

-Without any biases

-Without the expectation of confirming our initial impressions

-And using only the numbers

Having said that, what kind of market is Over? (Including Over 0.5).

Let me quote a chapter from "The Perfect Prediction," which not only explains how the Over market works in general but also introduces you to some analytical details that we will further delve into regarding Over 0.5:

A match characterized as an Over match generally has a final score of at least 3 goals (Over 2.5).

However, operating with Over does not necessarily mean betting that a match will end with more than 3 goals. This is because there are different Over markets, ranging from Over 0.5 (1 goal) to Over 6.5 (7 goals).

Fundamentally, the trick to successfully operate in these markets, which all share the same characteristic (winning when the match ends with more goals), is to be able to identify in advance, through the study of the two teams and the analysis of their statistics, if there is a strong MATHEMATICAL PREDISPOSITION to a certain number of goals scored per match.

As mentioned earlier, for a match to be defined as an Over match, there must be at least 3 goals scored.

But in reality, if we bet on Over 0.5, for example, we win even if the match ends with just a 1-0 scoreline.

The same applies to Over 1.5, where we win with 2 goals.

In these cases, we don't have to wait for all 3 goals to be scored in order to win our bet!

So, both operating on Over 0.5 and Over 1.5

are not only simpler because we need to predict fewer goals, but also have the advantage of betting on markets that can benefit from the overall trend of Over matches. (Since all matches that end in Over 2.5 are obviously also matches that fall under Over 0.5 and Over 1.5).

Now, let me ask you a question:

Do you think it's better to bet on Over 0.5 in a match that tends to be Under 2.5 statistically? In other words, a match that statistically tends to have fewer than 3 goals scored?

Or is it better to bet on Over 0.5 in a match that statistically tends to be Over 2.5?

It seems quite obvious that if you want to operate in any Over markets (especially Over 0.5 and 1.5), it is much better to choose a match that tends to have many goals rather than few. Therefore, matches that fall under Over 2.5!

To recap, in order to correctly predict a match for Over 0.5, you first need to be able to identify and select a match in advance that has a mathematical predisposition for Over 2.5 based on its statistics.

Matches to bet on are never chosen randomly, as casual bettors do.

Instead, it's important to always follow logic

and have a rational analysis criterion.

So now let's focus on the main aspect of this chapter: how to find a match for Over 2.5. What kind of characteristics does it have? What kind of calculations and considerations need to be made for such a match?"

1

First and foremost, an Over 2.5 match is not just a game between teams that score frequently; statistically, it is also a match between teams that often concede goals. Essentially, it is a game that strongly leans towards the Goal market (both teams score).

It is quite obvious that an Over match is usually also a Goal match. This is because if both teams score, there are more chances of reaching the required number of goals to win an Over bet compared to a situation where only one team scores.

To determine if the match at hand is one where both teams tend to score and concede goals, a general calculation can be done based on the last 5 matches played by both teams in their respective leagues, as well as their last 5 head-to-head encounters.

In general, it is better to focus on league matches and analyze only those. For statistical purposes, we are interested in the last 5 total matches, without considering whether they were played at home or away. The same applies to head-to-head encounters; we are concerned only with the last 5 matches played between the two teams, regardless of the venue.

For example, if the match in question is Aston Villa - Liverpool:

-At least 3 out of the last 5 total matches played by Aston Villa in the Premier League should have ended with both teams scoring

-At least 3 out of the last 5 total matches played by Liverpool in the Premier League should have ended with both teams scoring

-And at least 3 out of the last 5 total matches played between Aston Villa and Liverpool in the Premier League should have ended with both teams scoring

In other words, a minimum of 9 out of 15 matches must have been Goal matches.

This general calculation based on the last 5 total matches is an indicator to determine if a match has a predisposition towards the Goal market (both teams score). However, it is just a starting point, and additional analytical aspects will also be considered to assess the likelihood of Over 2.5 more accurately. These aspects include more detailed analysis of the *teams, playing styles, player absences, fitness conditions, and other influential factors.*

2

Once a mathematical predisposition to the Goal market is established, which is an essential factor to consider, the same calculation needs to be applied to the number of goals scored.

Specifically, we need to determine if:

-At least 3 out of the last 5 total matches played by Aston Villa in the Premier League have ended as Over 2.5, meaning a minimum of 3 goals were scored

-At least 3 out of the last 5 total matches played by Liverpool in the Premier League have ended as Over 2.5, meaning a minimum of 3 goals were scored

-And at least 3 out of the last 5 total matches played between Aston Villa and Liverpool in the Premier League have ended as Over 2.5, meaning a minimum of 3 goals were scored

Therefore, in this case as well, a minimum of 9 out of 15 matches must have ended as Over 2.5.

This calculation on the number of goals

scored further confirms the statistical tendency for a match to have a higher goal count. It provides additional evidence to support the selection of a match with a greater probability of meeting the Over 2.5 criterion. However, it is important to remember that this is just one aspect of the analysis, and other factors will also be taken into account to form a comprehensive assessment before making a prediction or placing a bet.

3

At this point, once we have established that the match we are analyzing has both a statistical probability of being a Goal match and an Over 2.5 match, we need to determine if the average goals scored by both teams is at least 3 goals per game.

The average goals are calculated as follows:

-Add up the number of goals scored in the last 5 matches by both teams (the same 5 matches we analyzed earlier)

-Divide the total by 5 (since we used 5 matches for this purpose)

-Sum up the three averages

-Divide the final result by 3 to obtain the overall average goals

For example, if Aston Villa has had the following results in their last 5 league matches:

1-2 = 3 goals 2-2 = 4 goals 0-3 = 3 goals 0-0 = 0 goals 3-4 = 7 goals

If we add up the total goals, we get: 17

Dividing 17 by 5 gives us: 3.4 (which means Aston Villa has an average of 3.4 goals per match in their last 5 total league matches).

We perform the same calculation for the last 5 total matches played by Liverpool, perhaps resulting in an average of 2.7 goals per match. Similarly, we calculate the average goals for the last 5 total league matches between Aston Villa and Liverpool, resulting in a final average of only 1.8 goals per match.

Adding 3.4 + 2.7 + 1.8 gives us 7.9

Dividing 7.9 by 3 gives us 2.6

In this case, since we have a final average of only 2.6 goals per match (which is less than 3), we DISCARD THIS MATCH because it is not considered sufficiently suitable for a strategy focused on the Over markets.

The first 3 points analyzed are technical and mathematical requirements NECESSARY to determine whether a match is suitable or not for an operational strategy on the Over markets.

Therefore, if a match fails to meet all 3 of these mandatory parameters, it will obviously be discarded.

However, if the statistics of the two teams do satisfy and perfectly align with what we are looking for in an Over match, we can still add some additional considerations:

-It helps if it is a match between a very strong team and a very weak team, meaning there is a clear difference in the values of the two teams. This is because an Over match is usually an unbalanced match

-It helps if the two teams are far apart in the league standings, but both are in excellent form

-It helps if it is not a Derby or a Big match, or generally a highly important match. This is because Over matches are usually played with ease and relaxation

-It helps if there have been no 0-0 draws in the recent matches

-It helps if it is not raining.

-It helps if there are no uncertain club situations, such as teams in a crisis of results, being up for sale, changes in coaches, major transfers, and so on.

To recap, the cornerstones of Over are 4:

1 A Goal match (both teams score)

2 An Over match (most of the recent matches have ended with more than 3 goals scored)

3 A definitive average of more than 3 goals per match

4 A great moment in the season for both teams.

THE FUNDAMENTALS OF OVER 0.5

I continue to quote "The Perfect Prediction" regarding the introduction to the Over 0.5 market and how to predict it:

The Over 0.5 market not only represents the simplest of all Over markets but also the easiest betting operation in football betting overall.

(Winning an Over 0.5 bet means betting that there will be at least one goal)

There are some bettors who have built their fortune with Over 0.5 bets. Now I'll explain how...

The mistake that many make when approaching this market, apart from randomly betting on Over 0.5 in any match without proper analysis, is to bet on Over 0.5 at the beginning of a match at very low odds, usually around 1.1 or even lower.

As explained in the previous chapters, you must always choose the appropriate matches. In this case, before formulating our Over 0.5 bet, we must always ensure that we have carefully selected a match suitable for the Over markets.
Therefore:

-Select a match with a mathematical predisposition for goals (both teams score)

-Select a match with a mathematical predisposition for Over 2.5

-A match with an average of at least 3 goals per game (as explained in the previous chapter)

So, never ever bet on Over 0.5 in a match that doesn't meet all three of these essential criteria!

That being said, another characteristic to consider, which applies only when predicting an Over 0.5 match, is that none of the last 5 matches of both teams have ended in a 0-0 draw.

For example, if we are still analyzing a hypothetical match (Aston Villa - Liverpool):

-None of the last 5 total matches played by Aston Villa in the league should have ended in a 0-0 draw

-None of the last 5 total matches played by Liverpool in the league should have ended in a 0-0 draw

-And none of the last 5 total direct encounters between Aston Villa and Liverpool in the league should have ended in a 0-0 draw

At this point, after finding a perfect match for an Over 0.5 bet, we just have to wait for the start of the game and hope that there are no goals in the first half.

As mentioned earlier, the odds cannot be too

low. Otherwise, statistically, it would take too many bets to recover for each loss...

So, the perfect odds for Over 0.5 should be at least 1.2 - Ideally 1.25. This means that for every loss, we only need to win 4 or 5 Over 0.5 bets to recover. That's not bad at all, considering that statistically, Over 0.5 can be successful at least 9 times out of 10.

In practice, we have to wait for the second half... Wait for the Over 0.5 odds to reach at least 1.25, and if there haven't been any red cards: BET ON OVER 0.5.

As I just explained, this strategy for Over 0.5 has statistically proven reliability of at least 9 out of 10 matches... But I want to emphasize that statistics make sense only with a large number of data points.

So, the more bets are made using this method, the more this statistic will have practical confirmation in its effectiveness. Don't expect to have 9 correct predictions out of the first 10, for example. Usually, statistics start to align after a minimum of 100 bets or more (which in this case would be around 90 winning bets).

And never forget that in betting, besides always betting the same amount and never doubling it when you lose (a very low amount that is less than 5% of the money you have available to bet), what plays an extremely important role is to blindly trust the strategy.

So, never ever bet on Over 0.5 in a match that doesn't meet all the requirements we've discussed...

Never ever bet on Over 0.5 at odds lower than 1.25.

And of course, also avoid other bets if, for example, the match in question becomes goal-scoring in the first half, and the Over 0.5 market is no longer available to play.

SUMMARY ON OVER 0.5

Before delving into the more technical aspects of this manual on Over 0.5 (which, all things considered, is more of a proper course than a book), I wanted to summarize all the key points we discussed earlier. This way, everything will be clearer.

First and foremost, before executing our Over 0.5 operation, we need to go through several decision-making steps. Firstly, we have to select a match based on its Over characteristics, and then verify that all the characteristics for Over 0.5 are present.

So, what are the Over characteristics?

1 Predisposition to the Goal market: At least 3 out of the last 5 TOTAL matches played in the league must have ended with both teams scoring. This applies to both the home team, the away team, and the head-to-head matches between the two teams. In other words, 9 out of 15 matches must have ended with goals.

2 Predisposition to the Over (2.5) market: At least 3 out of the last 5 TOTAL matches played in the league must have ended as Over 2.5. Again, this applies to both the home team, the away team, and the head-to-head matches between the two teams. In other words, 9 out of 15 matches must have ended as Over 2.5.

3 The average number of goals per match must be at least 3: To calculate this, we consider the goal averages of the last 5 TOTAL matches for the home team, the away team, and the head-to-head matches between the two teams. Finally, we calculate the overall average of these 3 goal averages. I reiterate: this final average must be higher than 3.

Once it is ensured that all three of these characteristics are present (it is crucial that none of these three points is missing), it is also necessary to verify that NONE OF THE LAST 5 TOTAL MATCHES PLAYED BY BOTH TEAMS, INCLUDING HEAD-TO-HEAD MATCHES, HAVE ENDED IN A 0-0 DRAW.

Regarding other more subjective considerations, it is certainly better if:

-It is a match between teams in good form

-It is a match between teams of different skill levels, preferably a top team against a much smaller club

-It is a league match, not a cup or international match

Once we have reached this point, further analysis of the statistics of the two teams is necessary (which we will discuss in the following chapters). And as I mentioned before, NEVER bet on Over 0.5 before the match starts, and never bet in the first half or at odds lower than 1.2/25

Regarding this market (once the right match to apply this strategy has been identified), it is always necessary to wait for the teams to start the second half with a score of 0-0. In that case, the odds for Over 0.5 will increase as the minutes pass, and consequently, become more advantageous, starting from odds of 1.25 and higher.

However, if a goal is scored before the second half begins, meaning the score is different from 0-0, any plans for an operation must be canceled, and one should wait for the next match compatible with the Over 0.5 strategy.

THREE EXAMPLES OF MATCHES TO DISCARD

When analyzing the statistics of a match to determine if all the key points of our strategy are present or not, it is advisable to start with the 0-0 results. This is because they can be easily identified, allowing us to quickly discard a match without delving into the more time-consuming and complex calculations of other statistics.

Lazio   Torino

18:00
Today
14:53:36

14/04/23 FT	Spezia	Lazio	0 3	W
08/04/23 FT	Lazio	Juventus	2 1	W
02/04/23 FT	Monza	Lazio	0 2	W
19/03/23 FT	Lazio	Roma x2	1 0	W
11/03/23 FT	Bologna	Lazio	0 0	D

For example, in the case of Lazio vs. Torino, as can be seen from the second image, in the last 5 matches played by Lazio in the league, the fifth result, which is the oldest one, is a 0-0 draw in a match played in Bologna. (In such a situation, the Lazio vs. Torino match can be immediately discarded as unsuitable for an Over 0.5 bet).

-Therefore, first, it is advisable to check if there are any matches that ended in a 0-0 draw (as it is the quickest check to perform)

-Once it is confirmed that there are no 0-0 draws, we can proceed to calculate the matches with goals and over 2.5

-Finally, and only if everything is in order, the average number of goals is calculated (which is the slowest and most complex analysis to perform)

Now let's analyze the match between Mainz and Bayern Munich, which will also take place on April 22, 2023, just like Lazio vs. Torino.

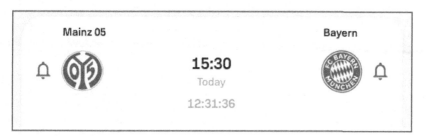

As you can see from the images, in this case, there are no 0-0 draws, and as for the matches with goals from both teams, there are no issues as almost all matches ended with goals (13 out of 15).

15/04/23 FT	Köln Mainz 05		1 1	D
08/04/23 FT	Mainz 05 Bremen		2 2	D
01/04/23 FT	Leipzig Mainz 05		0 3	W
19/03/23 FT	Mainz 05 Freiburg		1 1	D
11/03/23 FT	Hertha Mainz 05		1 1	D

15/04/23 FT	Bayern Hoffenheim		1 1	D
08/04/23 FT	Freiburg Bayern		0 1	W
01/04/23 FT	Bayern Dortmund		4 2	W
19/03/23 FT	Leverkusen Bayern		2 1	L
11/03/23 FT	Bayern Augsburg		5 3	W

29/10/22 FT	Bayern Mainz 05		6 2	🔔
30/04/22 FT	Mainz 05 Bayern		3 1	🔔
11/12/21 FT	Bayern Mainz 05		2 1	🔔
24/04/21 FT	Mainz 05 Bayern		2 1	🔔
03/01/21 FT	Bayern Mainz 05		5 2	🔔

The problem arises with matches over 2.5 goals. This is because Mainz did not achieve the minimum requirement of 3 out of 5 matches ending over 2.5 goals in their last 5 league matches.

In essence, even this match does not pass our

compatibility test for the over 0.5 strategy.

The same reasoning applies to the match between Borussia Dortmund and Frankfurt, which will also take place on April 22, 2023.

In this case as well, there are no 0-0 draws, and there have been 14 out of 15 matches with goals from both teams.

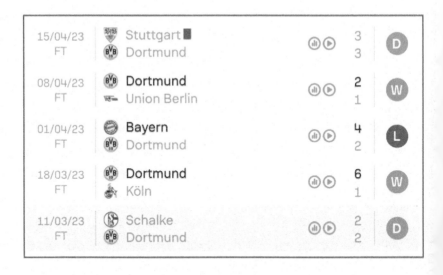

15/04/23 FT	Frankfurt M'gladbach		1 1	D
08/04/23 FT	Leverkusen Frankfurt		3 1	L
31/03/23 FT	Frankfurt Bochum		1 1	D
19/03/23 FT	Union Berlin Frankfurt		2 0	L
11/03/23 FT	Frankfurt Stuttgart		1 1	D

29/10/22 FT	Frankfurt Dortmund		1 2	🔔
08/01/22 FT	Frankfurt Dortmund		2 3	🔔
14/08/21 FT	Dortmund Frankfurt		5 2	🔔
03/04/21 FT	Dortmund Frankfurt		1 2	🔔
05/12/20 FT	Frankfurt Dortmund		1 1	🔔

Unfortunately, Frankfurt has only had one match out of their last 5 league matches that ended over 2.5 goals, which is insufficient.

43

REAL MADRID VS. CELTA VIGO - A CASE STUDY

When it comes to the Real Madrid vs. Celta Vigo match, we have all the parameters in place...

-There are no matches ending in a 0-0 draw

-10 out of 15 matches have seen both teams scoring goals

-12 out of 15 matches have ended with over 2.5 goals

21:00 -	Real Madrid Celta			🔔
15/04/23 FT	Cádiz Real Madrid	📊 ▶	0 2	W
08/04/23 FT	Real Madrid Villarreal	📊 ▶	2 3	L
02/04/23 FT	Real Madrid Valladolid	📊 ▶	6 0	W
19/03/23 FT	Barcelona Real Madrid	📊 ▶	2 1	L
11/03/23 FT	Real Madrid Espanyol	📊 ▶	3 1	W

21:00 -	Real Madrid Celta			🔔
17/04/23 FT	Celta ■ Mallorca	📊 ▶	0 1	L
07/04/23 FT	Sevilla ■ x2 Celta	📊 ▶	2 2	D
02/04/23 FT	Celta Almería	📊 ▶	2 2	D
18/03/23 FT	Espanyol Celta	📊 ▶	1 3	W
11/03/23 FT	Celta Rayo Vallecano	📊 ▶	3 0	W

21:00	Real Madrid			
–	Celta			
20/08/22	Celta		1	
FT	Real Madrid		4	
02/04/22	Celta		1	
FT	Real Madrid		2	
12/09/21	Real Madrid		5	
FT	Celta		2	
20/03/21	Celta		1	
FT	Real Madrid		3	
02/01/21	Real Madrid		2	
FT	Celta		0	

Furthermore, the overall goal average is 3.7 goals per match (we will discuss how to calculate the goal average in detail later, aided by a specific graphical representation that helps with further calculations).

Unlike the previous matches discussed in the previous chapter, this game deserves to be analyzed further and possibly considered for betting, as it currently possesses all the key and essential characteristics for our Over 0.5 strategy.

Unfortunately, the match ended 2-0, and to our regret, the first goal was scored towards the end of the first half, invalidating any potential bet on Over 0.5.

I would like to emphasize that the strategy we are discussing requires an ongoing match for the Over 0.5 odds to be advantageous for us as bettors and not for the bookmaker. For example, during the first half of Real Madrid vs. Celta Vigo, until the 30th minute, the odds for Over 0.5 were still below 1.1, which is too low.

Therefore, as explained in the introductory chapter, we must wait for the teams to still be tied 0-0 in the second half and, if appropriate, only after the second half starts and the odds reach a minimum of 1.25, place a bet on Over 0.5.

However, there are additional things to know about this, which I will discuss in the following chapters.

TECHNICAL ANALYSIS AND FUNDAMENTAL ANALYSIS

Everything we have discussed so far is not enough to guarantee consistent profits over time through the use of this strategy on Over 0.5 goals... This is because some key concepts of professional betting are missing.

Specifically, we need to differentiate (as trendy younger bettors say nowadays) between Technical Analysis and Fundamental Analysis of the match. And even more importantly, we need to consider Expected Value (EV), which quantifies the average outcome of each betting operation. But let's take it step by step...

In the realm of betting, everything related to numbers, match selection, and proper statistical analysis aimed at quantifying the value of each individual operation (EV) is commonly referred to as Technical Analysis. This term originates from the study of charts in financial markets.

On the other hand, Fundamental Analysis, also derived from the world of financial markets, refers to the study of a financial asset from a micro/ macro-economic perspective. In the context of betting, it means conducting Live Analysis during the match, assessing, based on how the two teams are interpreting the game, the likelihood of success or failure with a particular bet.

Technical Analysis

Up until this point, I have provided you with all the parameters and minimum requirements for selecting a suitable match for an Over operation, specifically Over 0.5. By the way, I have also explained that, on average, for an Over 0.5 operation, we must always wait for the odds to reach 1.25.

The reason for this is the existence of Expected Value (EV).

Let me explain. In the long run, after a series of X bets/operations on Over 0.5, more or less executed in the same manner with the same strategy, the correct decisions will have made us money, while the wrong ones will have caused us losses. However, thanks to the knowledge of the expected value of each individual bet we place (referred to as Expected Value), all of this becomes irrelevant. Because, if we've done the math correctly, over a minimum of 100 operations on average, we will always be in profit.

Expected Value is a mathematical concept that quantifies the average outcome of each individual operation. Let me explain further:

For example, let's say we bet on Inter's victory with odds of 2 in a match. We know that if Inter Milan wins, these odds will exactly pay us the same amount we bet. (In theory, it's like betting at a 50% probability, because 100/2 equals 50 - so 50%).

However, the odds given to us by the bookmaker at the beginning of the match, whether we like it or not, don't actually indicate that Inter Milan truly has a 50% chance of winning a particular game. It merely states that the payout is equivalent to what we would receive if Inter had a 50% chance of winning. In practice, it may not be the case.

Therefore, when it comes to betting, it is crucial to distinguish between the real odds of an event and its correct odds...

The real odds would be the actual odds that express the real probability of an event occurring. (And we have to calculate these odds ourselves; there is no other way to find it elsewhere, let alone on a sportsbook).

And the correct odds would be our real odds adjusted with a positive EV, which also represents the odds we have identified for placing our bet.

Now let's go back to the bet on Inter's victory with odds of 2.

Let's imagine that after calculating all the statistics, we discover that the real odds for this event are not 2, meaning that Inter doesn't have a 50% chance of winning but only a 30% chance! In this case, our real odds would be 3.3 (100/3.3 equals 30).

So, if we bet on an event with odds quoted at 50% (2) but should actually be quoted at 30% (3.3), it's evident that we are not making a good deal! We are betting on an event that, in case of a win, pays us much less than what we deserve to win. Therefore, we are operating with a negative EV of 20% (-50 + 30 = -20).

On the other hand, if, for instance, based on the statistics, we realize that the real odds for Inter's victory should be 1.75 (indicating a 57% chance of success), in this case, by betting at odds of 2, we already have a positive EV of 7 percentage points (-50 + 57 = 7).

Hence, if an action leads to a mathematical gain over time, we can say it has a positive expected value or EV+. Conversely, a losing operation in the long run has a negative expected value or EV-.

In the first case, betting with a negative EV of 20%, over 100 equal bets, we will experience an average loss of about 20% of our stake.

In the second case, with a positive EV of 7%, over 100 equal bets, we will achieve an average profit of about 7% of our stake.

However, betting with a 7% positive EV is not sufficient to achieve our goal of operating intelligently in the long run because a 7% correction relative to the real odds is too small!

Therefore, betting at correct odds means betting at real odds that are adjusted by at least 15 percentage points (with a positive EV of at least

15%).

In the second example we analyzed, where we said the real odds for Inter's victory were 1.75 (57%), to bet at correct odds with a 15% increase, we would need to place our bet at a probability of 42% (57 - 42 = 15). This corresponds to odds of at least 2.4.

Now, don't worry too much if you haven't fully understood these calculations because there will be opportunities in the future to discuss them in more detail and explain them specifically for an Over 0.5 operation using my strategy.

To conclude this subchapter on Technical Analysis, Pre-Live Analysis involves:

-All the parameters for match selection for Over and Over 0.5 (which we have already discussed)

-Detailed calculation of the Goal Average (which we will discuss in the next chapter)

-Calculation of the Mathematical Mode (which we will address later)

-Lastly, calculating the real odds, correct odds, and EV (to always know the minimum entry odds which for Over 0.5 are usually around 1.25)

Fundamental Analysis

After completing all the necessary technical analysis on a match to know EVERYTHING about the game (minimum requirements, details, and percentages), we simply have to wait for the match to start and hope that there are no goals in the first half.

Therefore, once the second half begins with a score of 0-0, depending on our correct odds with a 15% EV correction, we must start our hypothetical Fundamental Analysis of the live match to ultimately assess whether it is really advantageous to proceed with our Over 0.5 operation or not.

Fundamental Analysis serves to provide even more strength and credibility to the Technical Analysis conducted earlier. Betting without conducting Fundamental Analysis (i.e., without watching the match) based on the concept of real and correct odds and Expected Value would still yield a positive long-term return of at least 15%. However, with a good Fundamental Analysis, we can achieve a significantly higher average profit over 100 operations. By closely observing the match and not betting blindly, we will make fewer mistakes and consequently lose fewer bets.

This distinction between Technical Analysis and Fundamental Analysis in betting was introduced by the talented Italian bettor Gabriele Pro Betting. He is not only one of the world's leading experts in the Under-Over markets but also one of the few professional bettors who consistently demonstrate long-term profitability in betting.

THE GOAL AVERAGE

The Goal Average, which we discussed at the beginning of the book, is only needed during the match selection phase for our Over 0.5 strategy. It is crucial for us to categorically establish whether the Goal Average in a match exceeds 3 goals per game or not. However, this calculation alone is only partially sufficient...

Once we have determined that the match we are analyzing is compatible with our strategy and that the Goal Average is at least 3 goals per game, we need to move on to a much more elaborate calculation of the Goal Average (which will serve as a complement to other calculations later on).

The calculation of the Goal Average, as we discussed earlier, is based only on the last 5 total matches of the home team, the last 5 total matches of the away team, and the last 5 total head-to-head matches between the two teams (always considering league matches and excluding other competitions).

Now, the calculation will be performed in the same way but considering more combinations (still considering league matches). Specifically:

-The last 5 home matches of the home team

-The last 5 away matches of the away team

-The last 5 head-to-head matches between the two teams (home vs. away)

And...

-The last 5 total matches of the home team

-The last 5 total matches of the away team

-The last 5 total head-to-head matches between the two teams

And finally, before calculating the final Goal Average, we also need to calculate the Goal Average of the last two matches for all combinations. But let's take it step by step...

In this case, I have identified the match between Cologne and Bayern Munich, which will take place on April 27, 2023.

As you can see from the following images, this match already meets all the necessary requirements to proceed with our Technical Analysis...

27/05/23 15:30	Köln Bayern			🔔
20/05/23 FT	Bremen Köln	⏺⏵	1 1	D
12/05/23 FT	Köln Hertha	⏺⏵	5 2	W
05/05/23 FT	Leverkusen Köln	⏺⏵	1 2	W
29/04/23 FT	Köln Freiburg	⏺⏵	0 1	L
22/04/23 FT	Hoffenheim Köln	⏺⏵	1 3	W

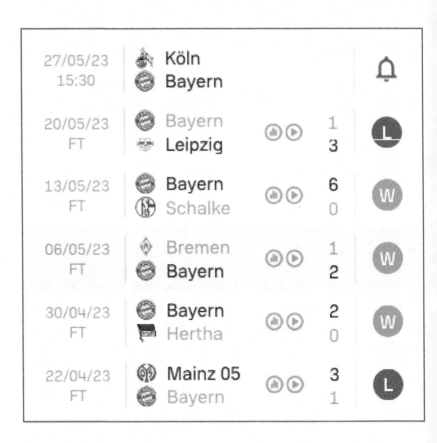

27/05/23 15:30	🛡 Köln 🔴 Bayern			🔔
20/05/23 FT	🔴 Bayern 🔴 Leipzig	⊙⊙	1 3	L
13/05/23 FT	🔴 Bayern 🔵 Schalke	⊙⊙	6 0	W
06/05/23 FT	⚪ Bremen 🔴 Bayern	⊙⊙	1 2	W
30/04/23 FT	🔴 Bayern 🏴 Hertha	⊙⊙	2 0	W
22/04/23 FT	🔴 Mainz 05 🔴 Bayern	⊙⊙	3 1	L

-No matches ended 0-0

-11 Goal matches

-11 Over matches

27/05/23 15:30	🦅 Köln ⚪ Bayern			🔔
24/01/23 FT	⚪ Bayern 🦅 Köln	📊 ▶	1 1	🔔
15/01/22 FT	🦅 Köln ⚪ Bayern	📊 ▶	0 4	🔔
22/08/21 FT	⚪ Bayern 🦅 Köln	📊 ▶	3 2	🔔

🔴 Club Friendly Games

███████████████████████ 🔔

▮ Bundesliga
Sofascore ratings

27/02/21 FT	⚪ Bayern 🦅 Köln	📊 ▶	5 1	🔔
31/10/20 FT	🦅 Köln ⚪ Bayern	📊	1 2	🔔

And a Goal Average of 3.7 goals per game...

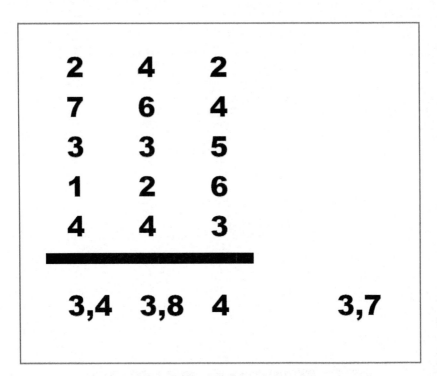

The left column represents the last 5 total matches played by Cologne in the league: starting from the top (which is the most recent match) and going downwards to the oldest match.

As you can see, on the first row of the left column, there is the number 2. (This is because the last Bundesliga match played by Cologne against Werder Bremen ended in a 1-1 draw (1 + 1 = 2).

On the second row of the left column, which is the second-to-last match played by Cologne, there is a 7. (This is because they won against Hertha Berlin with a score of 5-2 (5 + 2 = 7). And so on...

The center column represents the last 5 total matches played by Bayern Munich in the Bundesliga...

And the right column represents the last 5 total head-to-head matches between the two teams.

We have already discussed the calculation of the Goal Average. However, let's review it briefly: regarding the left column, 2+7+3+1+4 equals 17, divided by 5 = 3.4 (which means that Cologne has an average of 3.4 goals per game in their last 5 total matches).

The same calculation is done for all the columns, and in the end, we calculate the overall average among the averages of the three columns (3.4 + 3.8 + 4 equals 11.2 - Divided by 3 = 3.7). Thus, the Goal Average is 3.7 goals per game.

Now, at this point, we need to slightly complicate this calculation by adding another grid exactly like this one but considering only the respective HOME-AWAY matches. We will calculate the Goal Average of the last 5 matches played at home for the home team and the last 5 matches played away for the away team (as well as the last 5 head-to-head matches played HOME-AWAY).

Essentially, the calculation of the Goal Average "of the TOTALS" helps us understand the most recent performance of both teams (as they are the most recent matches). On the other hand, the Goal Average that only considers matches played HOME-AWAY helps us understand the behavior of the two teams in their respective home and away games.

Of course, some of the matches played HOME-AWAY are the same ones that will be calculated in the TOTAL matches, so they will be counted multiple times. But this is actually a good thing! These matches have more statistical value compared to others (primarily because they are more recent and secondly because they were played either at home or away, depending on where the match we are analyzing will take place).

HOME-AWAY			TOTAL		
7	3	4	2	4	2
1	4	3	7	6	4
2	1	5	3	3	5
0	3	4	1	2	6
2	3	3	4	4	3
───	───	───	───	───	───
2,4	2,8	3,8	3,4	3,8	4
	3			3,7	

Regarding the Goal Average of the respective last 5 HOME-AWAY matches, we have a lower average (compared to the TOTAL matches), which is "only" 3 goals per game.

Finally, let's also calculate the Average of the last 2 matches for all the columns (to give even more statistical value to the most recent games). We add up all the goals scored and divide them by 12 (since there are 2 matches for 6 columns).

HOME-AWAY			TOTAL		
7	3	4	2	4	2
1	4	3	7	6	4
2	1	5	3	3	5
0	3	4	1	2	6
2	3	3	4	4	3
▬▬▬					
2,4	2,8	3,8	3,4	3,8	4
	3			3,7	3,9

Since 47 (which is the sum of all the goals in the last 2 matches) divided by 12 equals 3.9 goals per game, we can confidently say that these two teams are experiencing a very positive trend in terms of "Over" matches. The averages of the most recent matches (the last 2) are higher than the other averages, and even higher than the overall average derived from all the averages (which is 3.5).

Ultimately, this is exactly the situation we always hope to see, the ideal situation. That is, a continuously increasing Goal Average from left to right and a Goal Average of the last 2 matches higher than the overall Goal Average.

Now, to complete the discussion on the Goal Average, we need to calculate the mathematical Mode of the match.

THE MATHEMATICAL MODE

The calculation of the Mathematical Mode is by far the most important calculation for our profession as professional bettors. It is through the final results of these calculations that we can have access to real statistical data and determine the actual odds on Over 0.5, thereby establishing the correct odds and potential positive Expected Value (EV).

The Mathematical Mode bridges the gap between the Goal Average and the final calculation of the actual and correct odds.

Let's take a closer look at what needs to be done:

We are still focusing on the same Colonia Bayern Monaco match, referring to the grids of our Goal Average calculations (at this point, knowing the Goal Average is no longer important for calculating the Mathematical Mode; we only need to know the number of goals scored in the last 5 matches for all combinations).

HOME-AWAY				TOTAL		
7	3	4		2	4	2
1	4	3		7	6	4
2	1	5		3	3	5
0	3	4		1	2	6
2	3	3		4	4	3

COLONIA - BAYERN MONACO

Therefore, we need to calculate:

-The number of matches that ended in a goalless draw (0-0) in all 30 cells, meaning in all 30 matches analyzed. (Of course, goalless draws will only be present in the grid of the left 15 matches, HOME-AWAY, and categorically never in the right grid, TOTAL, as this is one of the essential initial requirements)

-The number of matches that ended in a goalless draw (0-0) in the last 2 matches for all respective combinations. (Again, in this case, there might be matches that ended in a goalless draw only between the last 2 matches in the HOME-AWAY grid)

HOME-AWAY			TOTAL		
7	3	4	2	4	2
1	4	3	7	6	4
2	1	5	3	3	5
0	3	4	1	2	6
2	3	3	4	4	3

COLONIA - BAYERN MONACO

0 - 1   0 - 0

Hence, we write a 0 (to indicate matches that ended with 0 goals):

-On the left, a 1 (because there is only one match that ended in a goalless draw in both grids, resulting in a single 0-0 match in all 30 analyzed matches). I marked it in blue

-On the right, a 0 (because among the last 2 matches of all combinations, there is no match that ended in a goalless draw). I marked it in green

Next, we need to mark:

-The number of matches that ended with a single goal in all 30 cells

-The number of matches that ended with a single goal in the last 2 matches for both grids

HOME-AWAY			TOTAL		
7	3	4	2	4	2
1	4	3	7	6	4
2	1	5	3	3	5
0	3	4	1	2	6
2	3	3	4	4	3

COLONIA - BAYERN MONACO

0 - 1	0 - 0
1 - 3	1 - 1

We then write a 1 (to indicate matches that ended with 1 goal):

-On the left, a 3 (as there are 3 matches that ended with 1 goal, two in the left grid and one in the right grid)

-On the right, a 1 (because among the last 2 matches of all combinations, there is only one match that ended with 1 goal)

Finally, as the last step, we also need to mark:

-The number of matches that ended with 2 goals in all 30 cells

-The number of matches that ended with 2 goals in the last 2 matches for both grids

HOME-AWAY   **TOTAL**

7	3	4		2	4	2
1	4	3		7	6	4
2	1	5		3	3	5
0	3	4		1	2	6
2	3	3		4	4	3

COLONIA - BAYERN MONACO

0 - 1	0 - 0
1 - 3	1 - 1
2 - 5	2 - 2

We write 2 to indicate matches that ended with 2 goals:

-On the left, a 5 (as there are 5 matches that ended with 2 goals, two in the left grid and three in the right grid)

-On the right, a 2 (because among the last 2 matches of all combinations, there are two matches that ended with 2 goals)

Now, at this point, I would say we can stop here. Since we are only concerned with the Over 0.5 market - in this case, matches that end with at least one goal - matches that ended with 3 or more goals are not relevant and do not contribute to our statistics.

Essentially, since we are only interested in potentially betting on the Over 0.5 market (which typically represents an Under-type match), it is better to focus only on the statistics of matches that ended with Under 2.5 goals (or at most Over 1.5 goals).

On one hand, we have a selected match that meets the criteria for an Over match, with a Goal Average of over 3 goals per match, and even higher Goal Average for the last 2 matches (as we saw in the previous chapter).

On the other hand, we are about to statistically calculate the anomalous possibility that this match (on paper, an Over match) turns out to be an Under match, specifically, an Over 0.5 match.

0 - **1**	+	0 - **0**	=	(0)	**1**
1 - **3**	+	1 - **1**	=	(1)	**4**
2 - **5**	+	2 - **2**	=	(2)	**7**

So we add up the results from the three rows (marked in red). And we obtain:

1 + 0 = 1 for matches with (0) goals scored

3 + 1 = 4 for matches with (1) goal scored

5 + 2 = 7 for matches with (2) goals scored

What we need to know is that the results for (1) are always at least triple the number of matches with (0) goals.

In this case, we have a good difference of 3 times, which is excellent. (This means that statistically, if the match were to be initially blocked with no goals, there are 3 more chances for the match to open up and at least one goal to be scored before the end of the match.)

So please note that it is absolutely crucial for the matches with (1) goal to be at least triple (at a minimum!) the number of matches with (0) goals.

Another important aspect is that the number of goals in matches with (2) goals should be at least double (or close to double) the number of matches with (1) goal.

In this case, 7 is not exactly double the number of 4, but it is a difference of nearly double, which is acceptable.

In summary, what matters is that the results for (0) goals should be at most only one match! For example, never willingly accept to bet on Over 0.5 in a match that, according to the Mathematical Mode, has two or more results in matches with (0) goals.

In the next chapter, I will explain how you can convert these results into real, correct odds and percentage probabilities.

REAL ODDS AND CORRECT ODDS

We have finally reached the final phase of Technical Analysis, where we need to materialize all the numbers at our disposal and determine the concrete percentage probabilities of successfully predicting our Over 0.5 bet.

Let's go back to the Cologne vs. Bayern Munich match: we left off at the final results of the mathematical mode, which confirmed that Over 0.5 is about 4 times more likely than Under 0.5, and furthermore, that Over 1.5 is almost 8 times more likely than Under 0.5. But what does all this mean?

We have 1 game that ended with (0) goals.

We have 4 games that ended with (1) goal.

And we have 7 games that ended with (2) goals.

Let's sum up the quantity of these games that have been combined. So: 1 + 4 + 7 = 12.

In practice, we know that 12 is our reference point for calculating the accurate percentages we need (since 12 means there were 12 games that ended Under 2.5 - i.e., the games that represent our statistical anomaly that we need to consider).

So, on one hand, we have the number 12, and on the other hand, we have the number 1 (which represents the games that ended 0-0 and thus have (0) goals).

Now subtract the only game that ended without goals from 12:

12 - 1 = 11.

11 games ended Over 0.5.

Divide 11 by 12 to determine the percentage probability of a game ending with at least one goal.

11 divided by 12 equals 0.91 (multiplied by 100) = 91 - In other words, 91%.

This means that this game (even if it were to end Under 2.5) still has a 91% chance of ending with at least 1 goal scored.

So how do we calculate the real odds for this market operation? It's simple: we need to find the right combination so that dividing 100 by the odds gives us a 91% probability.

To round it off, in this case, let's say the real odds are 1.1 - because 100 divided by 1.1 equals 90.90.

So, in conclusion, is the odds of 1.1 high or low? The answer is that it is ONLY a real odds; it represents the actual statistical probabilities that a game like this, which initially seemed like an Under game after ending 0-0 in the first half, could actually end up being an Over 0.5 game instead of an Under 0.5 game.

But the problem is that by operating at real odds, on "for example" hundreds or thousands of bets, on average, it is difficult to make a profit (just as it is difficult to incur losses). This is because you are only betting at a fair market odds, which, in the long run, does not offer any statistical advantage or disadvantage.

In practice, you should always bet at a minimum but CORRECT real odds of at least 15 percentage points (as explained earlier).

So, with a real odds of 1.1 at 91% - Since 91 minus 15 equals 76, we should bet at a minimum of 76% probability percentage, which corresponds to odds of 1.3.

100 divided by 1.3 equals 76.

In the past, I indicated a minimum odds of 1.25 for performing the Over 0.5 operation. But that was just an example to introduce you to the importance of betting at a more accurate odds than usual.

In this case, according to the statistics we have seen and analyzed, for Over 0.5, odds of 1.25 are not sufficient (as it would imply betting at an 80% probability). Therefore, only with an EV+ of just 11 points...

For this game, the real odds for Over 0.5 are 1.1.

And the correct odds are at 1.3. So, never bet at lower odds.

Technical Analysis is finished!

However, let's continue talking about calculations, percentages, and real odds a bit more. And maybe we can do a few more calculation exercises together (using imaginary statistics). Because I want to make sure that everything is clear to you!

For example, let's pretend that the "imaginary" match between Lille and PSG has the following results based on the mathematical mode:

(0) 1

(1) 5

(2) 12

So, 18 total games, minus one game that ended 0-0.

17 divided by 18 equals 0.94 (94%).

Real odds: 1.06 (94%).
100/1.96 = 94

Correct odds: 1.26 (79%).
94-79 = 15
100/1.26 = 79

Now, let's assume that the "imaginary" match between Barcelona and Osasuna has the following results based on the mathematical mode:

(0) 0

(1) 4

(2) 9

So, 13 total games, but zero games ended 0-0.

According to this mathematical reasoning, we have a 100% probability that the game will end Over 0.5. But obviously, this is not possible! And since there is always a chance for a game to end goalless, in these cases, I calculate the real odds at a 98% probability.

Real odds: 1.02 (98%).
100/1.02 = 98.

Correct odds: 1.2 (83%).
98-83 = 15
100/1.2 = 83

In general, I always consider odds of 1.2 too low for Over 0.5. As far as I'm concerned, it's always better to start from a base of 1.25, which corresponds to 80%.

An operation with odds of 1.25 for a game with such statistics gives us a statistical advantage and a positive EV of 18 percentage points.

The examples I've given you, although invented, always reflect the requirements necessary to adhere to our strategy on Over 0.5. I hope you understand that it is a winning strategy from a mathematical standpoint in the long run. And I'm very proud of it! Now you can take advantage of it too!

CONCLUSION

Now let's conclude everything with some important final considerations...

As I explained before, this strategy can only work if, once you have made the decision to bet on Over 0.5 (always applying the strategy perfectly and following all the points), you do not change your mind once the operation is formulated.

So, once you have placed your bet, there's no going back! The second half lasts 45 minutes, plus any added time. We should not expect the goal to come immediately or that the teams always play at their maximum potential just because we bet on Over 0.5. We must always have faith in our strategy and consider that the statistics we have analyzed earlier are percentages taken from matches that lasted over 90 minutes, not 5-minute games.

In practice, it is absolutely detrimental to change your mind based on how the teams are playing, or even worse, based on how you feel at that moment...

f, in my career as a bettor, I had the habit of changing my mind about bets just because I was no longer sure I made the right choice, not only would I not be rich now, but I would have lost millions!

I'm not saying that you can't have doubts; they will always be there... But the doubt of whether to place a bet or not must be resolved BEFORE formulating the bet, not discussed afterwards!

So, I repeat: it must be the NUMBERS and STATISTICS that tell us whether the Over 0.5 operation can be done and is profitable in the long run or not.

If you happen to lose (and you should only lose at the end of the match, so never cash out just because the goal hasn't come yet), it's okay! You have to accept it and move on. It's impossible to win every operation.

The important thing is to make all the right calculations and always bet in the second half at the correct odds with an EV+ of at least 15%.

As for Fundamental Analysis, which some consider essential and others not (for me, less so), it is enough to see that the match is quite open and interesting in the second half, so that we can be more confident in betting on Over 0.5.

There may be cases where the match is completely blocked and very boring, and in that case, it may be appropriate to avoid betting (while waiting for a more eventful match in the future).

At this point, I can only advise you to READ this

text again. There might be points that you missed, but in general, I still recommend rereading this book regardless.

And most importantly: write down on a piece of paper all the minimum requirements for selecting a match for Over 0.5, and also note down all the things you need to calculate when performing Technical Analysis of a match.

Don't rely on memory! Especially if you're just starting out. Once you become familiar with this strategy, it will become automatic and easier, but for now, go through all the necessary steps methodically and thoughtfully.

I wish you great success and lots of money, Pavel.

Printed in Great Britain
by Amazon

42976748R00056